Sing My Song
A KID'S GUIDE TO SONGWRITING

Starring **Steve Seskin** and a chorus of creative kids

Illustrated by Eve Aldridge, Shino Arihara, Bob Barner, Tatjana Mai-Wyss, Jenny Mattheson, Frank Morrison, and Marissa Moss

TRICYCLE PRESS
Berkeley / Toronto

This book is dedicated to my wife, Ellen, and my son, David. Without your love and support, I couldn't do what I do. You're in every one of these songs as much as I am.   —SS

Acknowledgements

I would like to thank all the children who helped write these songs for their courage, enthusiasm, and creativity. I also want to acknowledge all the teachers who work hard every day to make this world a better place by educating and enriching the lives of our youth. A special thank you to art, music, dance, and drama teachers everywhere for encouraging kids to express themselves. In a world where standardized testing is leaving many children behind, it's never been more important to educate the whole child.

To the kids at Gomes Elementary School: Thanks for all your hard work singing these songs for the recording. You all did a great job! Special thanks to Marilyn Williams and Christina Broadwin for all their time and dedication while working with the kids at Gomes. Thanks to Music for Minors for bringing music programs to children all across the San Francisco Bay Area.

Thanks to David Decuir for recording and mixing, and hats off to all the incredible illustrators who contributed to this book. Keep up the great work! Thanks also to Terri Mazurek for coming up with a fabulous title.

Thanks to Summer, Joanne, Nicole, Laura, Betsy, and all the staff at Tricycle Press for their dedication to producing fabulous books for kids.

Last, a big thank you to all the kids and teachers at the following schools for their invaluable contribution to this collection:

Brett Elementary, Tamworth, NH ("Good Morning")

Chinook Elementary, Vancouver, WA ("My Dog")

Freedom Elementary, Tamworth, NH ("My Chicken")

Gomes Elementary, Fremont, CA ("A World Without Family," "Four Rs," "Read About It")

Hough Elementary, Vancouver, WA ("School Spirit")

King Elementary, Vancouver, WA ("Dreams and Nightmares")

Madison Elementary, Tamworth, NH ("If I Had a Million Dollars," "My Pets")

Pattengill Elementary, Ann Arbor, MI ("We're All Different")

Searles Elementary, Union City, CA ("You Are What You Eat")

Tricycle Press
an imprint of Ten Speed Press
PO Box 7123
Berkeley, California 94707
www.tricyclepress.com

Design by Betsy Stromberg
Typeset in Beton, Bell Gothic, Latiara, and Spoleto
The illustrations in this book were rendered in acrylic, collage, gouache, mixed media, oil, and watercolor.

Library of Congress Cataloging-in-Publication Data

Seskin, Steve.
  Sing My Song / by Steve Seskin ; illustrated by Eve Aldridge ... [et al.].
    p. cm.
Summary: An illustrated collection of songs co-written with children, with detailed instructions about the creative process of songwriting.
  ISBN-13: 978-1-58246-266-0 (hardcover)
  ISBN-10: 1-58246-266-6 (hardcover)
  1. Popular music–Writing and publishing–Juvenile literature. I. Barner, Bob, ill. II. Title.

  MT67.S42 2008
  782.42164'13–dc22

                                              2007046966

First Tricycle Press printing, 2008
Printed in Singapore

1 2 3 4 5 6 — 13 12 11 10 09 08

Contents

About the *Illustrators*

Eve Aldridge ("You Are What You Eat," "School Spirit") learned to draw, paint, and cut up tiny little pieces of paper at the California College of Arts, where she earned her BFA in Illustration. Her picture books include *Sarah's Story* by Bill Harley, and *Hurry Granny Annie* by Arlene Alda. When she's not illustrating, she's writing and reading children's books, staring at crossword puzzles, or running hills with her dog. Eve, her husband, and their dog live in Oakland, California.

Shino Arihara ("A World Without Family," "Dreams and Nightmares") is the illustrator of *Ceci Ann's Day of Why.* Her editorial illustrations have appeared in numerous publications including *Time* and *Boston Globe*. Shino lives in Pasadena, California, with her pianist husband and their many musical instruments.

Bob Barner ("My Pets," "My Chicken," "My Dog") has written and illustrated over 25 books, including *Penguins, Penguins, Everywhere; Fish Wish;* and *Dinosaur Bones*. His books have been translated into Korean, Spanish, and French, and also set to music and made into short films. He enjoys speaking to young readers at schools and libraries around the world. To find out more, visit www.bobbarner.com.

Tatjana Mai-Wyss ("If I Had a Million Dollars," "Read About It") was born in Switzerland. Growing up with her nose in a book, she always wanted to be the one to draw the pictures. Today Tatjana is a freelance illustrator in sunny South Carolina, where she lives with her husband and two musical daughters. She is the illustrator of *The Yawn Heard 'Round the World* and *That's Not How You Play Soccer, Daddy!*

Jenny Mattheson ("Good Morning") is a Pennsylvania native and received her BFA from The Art Institute of Boston. She is the illustrator of numerous books for children including *The Mouse, the Cat, and Grandmother's Hat; Christmas Morning; Happy to be Girls; No Bows;* and *Mrs. O'Leary's Cow*. She lives in Berkeley, California.

Frank Morrison ("We're All Different") was born in Massachusetts and grew up in New Jersey, where he was inspired by the music of neighborhood DJs and the colorful "tags" of local graffiti artists. He began painting at a very early age, and he is now the illustrator of many books for children including *Jazzy Miz Mozetta*, for which he won the Coretta Scott King/John Steptoe Award for New Talent, and *Sweet Music in Harlem*. To find out more, visit www.morrisongraphics.com.

Marissa Moss ("Four Rs") is an award-winning writer and illustrator best known for her *Amelia's Notebook* series, which has sold over five million copies and has been translated into four languages. Her other books include *Rachel's Journal: the Story of a Pioneer Girl* and *Hannah's Journal*, both featured in California state textbooks. Her picture book, *Jackie Mitchell, the Strike-Out Queen* (illustrated by C.F. Payne) was named a 2004 ALA Notable book.

Introduction

For the last four years I've visited schools all over North America to teach elementary school kids how to write songs. This book is a collection of a few of my favorites. Writing these songs has been an incredible learning experience for me as well as for the students. On these pages you can see and hear what happens when a group of people open up and get creative together. These songs are just the beginning.

I believe that with a few tools, anyone can write a song. Through the instructions in this book and on the audio CD, you will learn how to:

- Come up with a title and a topic for your song.

- Create a list of words for your lyrics.

- Write a chorus, verse, bridge, and tag for your song.

- Distinguish between different forms of songs.

- Use emotion and imagery in your lyrics.

- Create rhymes and imitate rhyme patterns in a song.

- Choose music to enhance the theme of your song.

I love writing songs. It's a great way to share a message and let people know how you feel about something. I think of each song as a gift to the world. My hope is that after you read this book, you will be inspired to express yourself through a song of your own.

Music Terms

BRIDGE (BR): the part of a song that offers another point of view lyrically while introducing a new musical figure

CHORD: a combination of three or more notes sounded at the same time

CHORUS (CH): a line or group of lines repeated two or more times in a song containing the song's central theme

LYRICS: the words of a song

MELODY: a pleasing arrangement of sounds that makes up a musical phrase

RHYME: a word that corresponds with another in sound, especially at the end

TAG (T): the tail end of a song that often repeats the title for emphasis

VERSE (VS): the descriptive part of a song often used to illustrate the message of the chorus

Note: Abbreviations (BR, CH, VS, T) have been used on the lyrics pages to indicate the parts of the song. "VS 1" stands for "Verse 1," "VS 2" stands for "Verse 2," etc.

Good Morning

I was performing for 400 kids at a school assembly when I said, "Good morning!" to everyone. All of them responded with a big "Good morning!" back to me. That's when I had the idea to write a call-and-response song with them, where the audience repeats portions of the song (kind of like an echo).

VS 1

Good morning! (Good morning!)
How are you? (How are you?)
Did ya get some sleep (Did ya get some sleep)
Last night? (Last night?)

VS 2

Good morning! (Good morning!)
Are ya ready? (Are ya ready?)
To have a great day (To have a great day)
Do what's right (Do what's right)

BR

How was your ride on the bus?
Did you remember your lunch?
Did you brush your teeth after breakfast?
Did you give your mom a kiss goodbye?

VS 3

Good morning! (Good morning!)
You're looking good (You're looking good)
I like your shoes (I like your shoes)
I like your hair (I like your hair)

VS 4

Good morning! (Good morning!)
Pay attention (Pay attention)
To your teacher (To your teacher)
Play fair (Play fair)

BR

Be nice to me and I'll be nice to you
Yeah, I'll be your friend if you'll
  be mine, too
If we all work together
This school will be much better

T

Good morning! (Good morning!)
Good morning! (Good morning!)
Good morning! (Good morning!)
To you!

You *Are* What You *Eat*

The kids and I enjoyed making a list of our favorite foods for this song. (The only problem was that some of us got pretty hungry!) Notice that the last word of the two verses, "you," is repeated in the first word of the following chorus. We decided to stretch out the word to "yooouuuu" so that we only sing it once, which makes that part especially fun to sing. Try to find the other song in this book where we do the same thing.

VS 1

I like my french fries with lots of ketchup
I love apple pie with vanilla ice cream
I like Twinkies and Ho Hos, Skittles
    and Cheetos
Pizza and hamburgers, too
They taste good but they're not that good
    for you

CH

You are what you eat
So try to think about what you put in
    your mouth
If you want to grow up to be strong
    and tough
Make sure you get enough of the good stuff

VS 2

Like grilled salmon and a big salad
A little bit of broccoli and mashed potatoes
Strawberries, raspberries, blackberries,
    blueberries
Carrots and celery, too
They taste good and they're good for you

CH

You are what you eat
So try to think about what you put in
    your mouth
If you want to grow up to be strong
    and tough
Make sure you get enough of the good stuff

BR

Now I'm not saying I won't be eating
    mac and cheese
Pass the cookies, please
But if all I ate was fat and sweets
My heart might stop
My teeth would rot
And where would that leave me?

CH

You are what you eat
So try to think about what you put in
    your mouth
If you want to grow up to be strong
    and tough
Make sure you get enough of the good stuff

T

And next time you reach for a treat,
    remember
You are what you eat

If I Had a *Million* Dollars

To get our ideas flowing, we first made a list of all the things that the kids would buy if they had a million dollars. From there we talked about how we might use the money to help people. These ideas became the verses for our song. Then we wrote a bridge to sum up the good feelings we get from giving to others. Try writing a verse about what you would do if you had a million dollars.

VS 1

If I had a million dollars
I'd buy a boat and a jet, a limo
A four-wheeler and a park
I'd get a monkey, a tiger, a beluga whale
And a great white shark

VS 2

If I had a million dollars
I'd help the poor, I'd make sure everybody
Had enough to eat
I'd give some to my mom, a little to my
   teacher
And I'd help people on the street
That's what I'd do
If I had a million dollars

BR

And I have to say that it seems to me
That the more I give away
The happier I'll be

VS 3

If I had a million dollars
I'd help my school, that'd be cool,
   we'd have a pool
And a brand new yellow bus
The music room would have some drums,
   more guitars
And Miss Walker would have an assistant
   named Gus
Yeah, that's what I'd do
If I had a million dollars
That's what I'd do
If I had a million dollars

My Pets

The sound effects for this song just happened as we started singing. My favorites are the "hissss" of the snake and the "owww!" from the turtle bite. Notice how the chorus offers general thoughts about the pets we love, and the verses describe specific pets and something special about each one.

VS 1

I've got a dog who rolls over
　　(arff, arff, arff...)
A cow that goes, "Moo!"
I have a cat who likes to jump from trees
　　(meow)
And some chickens in a coop
　　(bawk, bawk, bawk...)

VS 2

I've got a snake who likes to slither
　　(hissssssss)
Some fish who love to swim (ooohhh)
A hamster, a lizard, and a robin that's
　　too thin

CH

My pets, my pets!
I play with them
My pets, my pets!
I take care of them
And they love me
And it's easy to see
I love my pets, my pets

VS 3

Now it's my job to feed them
Give them water and teach them tricks
　　(whee!)
I go with my mom to the vet
Whenever they get sick (oh no!)

VS 4

I play fetch and Frisbee with my dog
　　(arff, arff, arff...)
I like to chase my pig (oink, oink, oink...)
One time I picked my turtle up
And he bit me on the lip (owww!)

CH

My pets, my pets!
I play with them
My pets, my pets!
I take care of them
And they love me
And it's easy to see
I love my pets, my pets

T

My pets, my pets
My pets, my pets

My Chicken

At one of my school visits, I met a little girl who said that her parents wouldn't let her have a dog, so she decided to make one of the family chickens her pet and named it "Fluffy." This song is dedicated to Fluffy, the chicken.

VS 1
My chicken likes to listen to the radio
And dance around the yard on just one leg
He says, "Cock-a-doodle-doo!"
And sometimes eats my shoe
And once in a while
He lays eggs

VS 2
My chicken likes to eat a lot of junk
He fluffs up his feathers sometimes
He pecks and he goes, "Bawk!"
I swear I heard him talk
And for the most part he is kind

BR
And I love my chicken
He means the world to me
I'm crazy 'bout my chicken
That's easy to see

VS 3
My chicken likes to listen to the radio
And dance around the yard on just one leg
He says, "Cock-a-doodle-doo!"
And sometimes eats my shoe
And once in a while
He lays eggs

T
My chicken (my chicken)
My chicken (my chicken)
My chicken

My Dog

Of all the titles I've written with kids, this one is by far the most popular. Over the years, I've written many versions of "My Dog." This one is my favorite because it has some really funny lines (and because I have two big labs of my own that act a lot like the dog described in this song).

VS 1

My dog has hair
Yeah, he's quite rare
He chases my cat around the room
He barks for no reason
Sometimes he freaks out
And he likes to chew on my mom's broom

CH

He protects me
He's my best friend
And I'm gonna love him
'Til the end of time

VS 2

My dog eats like a hog
He sleeps like a log
He weighs one hundred pounds
No, he's no Chihuahua
No little weenie dog
He's a big old lazy hound

CH

He protects me
He's my best friend
And I'm gonna love him
'Til the end of time

BR

And he's fun to play with
He can hold three things in his mouth
And when I'm at school I miss him
A lot

CH

He protects me
He's my best friend
And I'm gonna love him
'Til the end of time
'Til the end of time

A *World* Without *Family*

For this song, we decided to use the title in the first line of the chorus. After we came up with a title, I asked everyone "what kind of world would that be?"—which became the second line of the chorus. The words for a song come when you ask yourself questions, and share how you really feel about something.

VS 1

I had a dream last night that really scared me
I was alone in this world, I had no family
No father no mother no sisters no brothers
No one to cheer me up
No one to cook breakfast
No help with my homework
No one to wish me luck

CH

A world without family
What kind of world would that be?
No one to stand by my side
No one to care about me
A world without happiness
Just sorrow and loneliness
It doesn't sound that good to me
A world without family

VS 2

They give me good advice and
    encouragement
My parents listen to me, they're my
    best friends
I love my aunts and my uncles and
    most of my cousins
And let me make one thing clear
When it comes to my parents
Without them, I wouldn't even be here

CH

A world without family
What kind of world would that be?
No one to stand by my side
No one to care about me
A world without happiness
Just sorrow and loneliness
It doesn't sound that good to me
A world without family

T

A world without family
I had a dream last night that really
    scared me

Four Rs

CH 1

It's good for the bottle, it's good for the can
Recycling is good for every child,
    every woman, every man
We all have to do our part
And this is how you start

VS 1

Start a compost bin
Throw your egg shells in
Your fruit peels, your tea leaves,
    and the grass that you mow
Maybe some vegetables, maybe some
    coffee grounds
And when it all breaks down it will help
    your garden grow

CH 2

Reuse (reuse)
Reduce (reduce)
Recycle (recycle)
Rot!

CH 1

It's good for the bottle, it's good for the can
Recycling is good for every child,
    every woman, every man
We all have to do our part
And it's high time that we start

VS 2

'Cause if we don't do it now
I can't imagine how
This world will be around forever
So don't litter, don't waste, it's not too late
    and we're all in this together

CH 2

Reuse (reuse)
Reduce (reduce)
Recycle (recycle)
Rot!

BR

It's a solution to all this pollution
I've thought about it and I've come to
    this conclusion

CH 1

It's good for the bottle, it's good for the can
Recycling is good for every child,
    every woman, every man
We all have to do our part
And now you know how to start

CH 2

Reuse (reuse)
Reduce (reduce)
Recycle (recycle)
Rot!

Read About It

I was in a school library with a bunch of students when I noticed signs everywhere that said "Read About It." The students and I started talking about how enjoyable and important it is to read, and the song just grew from there. Can you find the parts of this song that rhyme? Try writing a different second verse listing some of your favorite books.

When I want to know about it, I read about it
A book can take you on a trip
A book can make you feel

CH
It's a magnificent adventure of people
   and places
It's more than words on pages
It's make believe and real
When I want to know about it, I read about it

VS 1
It's Math and Science
The English language
Geography
Social Studies, Art and Music
World History
I love to read
I love the library

When I want to know about it, I read about it
A book can take you on a trip
A book can make you feel

CH
It's a magnificent adventure of people
   and places
It's more than words on pages
It's make believe and real
When I want to know about it, I read about it

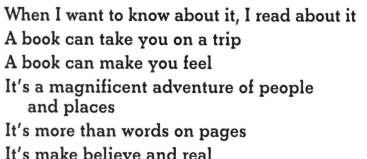

VS 2
There's a cover, there's a title
A beginning and an end
There's an author, an illustrator
Books are my best friend
It's fun to read
It's no mystery

When I want to know about it, I read about it
A book can take you on a trip
A book can make you feel

CH
It's a magnificent adventure of people
   and places
It's more than words on pages
It's make believe and real
When I want to know about it, I read about it

T
I read about it
I read about it

We're *All* Different

We purposely wrote a simple chorus with two lines that repeat, which encourages the listener to sing along. The verses go into detail, helping to illustrate the chorus by pointing out ways that we're all different and the same. Notice that the last chorus is sung without instruments playing. This type of singing is called "a cappella."

CH
We're all different on the outside
But on the inside we're all the same
We're all different on the outside
But on the inside we're all the same

VS 1
We're a rainbow of colors
Come in many shapes and sizes
We're kinda like M&Ms
You speak your language and I speak mine
But that doesn't mean we can't be friends

CH
We're all different on the outside
But on the inside we're all the same
We're all different on the outside
But on the inside we're all the same

VS 2
We come from many countries
All kinds of religions
But we all have a heart and a brain
We all want to be happy
All want to feel safe
And we've all felt joy and pain

CH
We're all different on the outside
But on the inside we're all the same
We're all different on the outside
But on the inside we're all the same

CH
We're all different on the outside
But on the inside we're all the same
We're all different on the outside
But on the inside we're all the same
We're all the same

Dreams and Nightmares

It's always a good idea to keep a notebook for your thoughts. For this song, the students and I jotted down more ideas than we could fit into one song. This meant that we had to leave some things out and choose only the most colorful ideas for the lyrics. You never know when the words you leave out will inspire you to write your next song. . . .

CH

Dreams and nightmares, dreams and
    nightmares
Some make you happy, some make you sad
Some are so scary, some are good,
    some are bad
Dreams and nightmares

VS 1

I had a dream last night
I was the fairy in fairyland
I was flying over Alaska when Pokémon
    came to life
I was a ballerina
I was an army soldier
Then my dad caught three wild horses for
    me and my sister and him to ride

CH

Dreams and nightmares, dreams and
    nightmares
Some make you happy, some make you sad
Some are so scary, some are good,
    some are bad
Dreams and nightmares

VS 2

I had a nightmare last night
I was falling off of the Empire State Building
An alligator tried to eat my breakfast—
    I said, "Hey, that's mine!"
Someone was trying to hurt my mom
A ghost scared me half to death
There were creepy crawlies in my bed
I woke up just in time!

CH

Dreams and nightmares, dreams and
    nightmares
Some make you happy, some make you sad
Some are so scary, some are good,
    some are bad
Dreams and nightmares

T

Dreams and nighmares
Dreams and nightmares....

School Spirit

When I hear this song, it makes me want to go to a school where people care about each other and help each other out. Listen to how the music in this song really captures the energy of the words.

VS 1
This morning I got to school
Someone wasn't being cool
Moping around, head to the ground
Bringing me down

VS 2
I said "Can you use a hand?"
I said "Can I be a friend?"
"What's on your mind?"
I'm trying to be kind
Trying to help you find

CH
Some school spirit
Express yourself
Be a role model for somebody else
Work hard, play fair
And never give up, show someone you care
With kindness and love
Show some school, school spirit

VS 3
I was eating my lunch when
I saw that person again
Playing in the sun
Having so much fun
They hit a home run

VS 4
That's when I knew I could
Make somebody else feel good
Maybe someday I'll feel that way
And someone will say

CH
Show some school spirit
Express yourself
Be a role model for somebody else
Work hard, play fair
And never give up, show someone you care
With kindness and love

CH
Show some school spirit
Express yourself
Be a role model for somebody else
Work hard, play fair
And never give up, show someone you care
With kindness and love
Show some school, school spirit
School Spirit!

How to *Write a Song*

Now that you've seen what other kids have created, it's time for you to give songwriting a try.

Title & Topic

The easiest way to begin is to come up with a title and a topic. Think of people, places, events, or things that are important to you. Use your imagination. What's been going on in your world lately? If you are having trouble starting, choose a title from the book and write your own song to go with it. Have a dog? Use "My Dog." Or try "School Spirit" and write about what your school is like.

Lists

Once you've chosen a title, it's time to make a few lists. These lists will contain everything you can think of about your title's topic and will contain many of the words you use to write your song. I'll use "You Are What You Eat" as an example. First, the class and I came up with some general ideas: Think about what you eat. Try to eat healthy foods. Eat some fun foods that taste great.

Next, we made two lists of foods—one for foods that we all like to eat (but that are not necessarily healthy,) and the other for foods that are good for us. We tried to use very specific words like "Ho Hos" and "Twinkies" instead of just "candy," or "carrots and celery" instead of just "vegetables." But these words are not complete lyrics. The next step is to turn the list of words into sentences that will become your lyrics.

Most songs have three different sections: the Chorus, the Verse, and the Bridge.

Chorus

The CHORUS is the part of a song you sing over and over, usually two or three times. It contains thoughts that summarize what the song is about. The title of the song is often in the chorus. Here's the chorus of "Dreams and Nightmares":

Dreams and nightmares, dreams and nightmares
Some make you happy, some make you sad
Some are so scary, some are good, some are bad
Dreams and nightmares

The chorus is usually the first section I write. I think of it as a road map that tells me where the song is going. I find it easier to stay on track when I'm writing the verses if I can refer back to the chorus.

Verse

VERSES provide the details of a song, and there are usually at least two or three verses in each song. Even though the music that accompanies each verse stays the same, the words change. When writing a verse, you should use very specific words and descriptive adjectives to help illustrate your point. I use a technique called "show me, don't tell me." Don't tell me how you feel, paint me a picture that makes me feel that same way.

One job of the verse is to bring new meaning to the chorus each time the listener hears it. So even though the words of the chorus are always the same, they take on different meanings as the song goes on. In "Dreams and Nightmares" the verses describe in detail the happy, sad, scary, good, and bad dreams that are mentioned in the chorus. It made sense to write one verse about dreams and one verse about nightmares. We could have mixed a little of each into both verses but chose to keep them separate.

In "You Are What You Eat," the first verse is packed with foods we love to eat but that are bad for our bodies. Since the chorus ends with "make sure you get enough of the good stuff," we decided to include in the second verse the salmon, broccoli, strawberries, and other healthy foods from our list.

Another job of the verse is to move the story along and show how time is passing. "Good Morning" begins at home, and describes getting ready for school. The second verse takes place later in the day at school. One thing you don't want is to hear two verses that repeat the same theme with different words. To avoid this, develop two or three different perspectives, or points of view, for your verses. Keep your listener interested for the whole song by creating a journey that never gets boring.

Bridge

The BRIDGE, which is usually only two to four lines, offers a fresh look at the subject that hasn't been addressed in the verse or chorus. In "You Are What You Eat," the lyrics of the bridge ("I'm not saying...") explain that a little junk food is okay but too much can be dangerous. But not all songs have a bridge. I only write one when I have a little left to say. If I have a lot more to say, I write another verse. Musically, it should be a unique section to make it stand out from the rest of the song.

Tag

A TAG is a short section at the end of a song that is used for emphasis. It either repeats the title a few times (like in "Good Morning,") or introduces a new closing thought (like in "You Are What You Eat").

Song Forms

There are many forms to songs. Some start with the verse, some start with the chorus. Some songs, like "If I Had a Million Dollars," have no chorus at all, but use the title in the beginning or end of the verse. Following are some choices for your song form. (Note that a tag may be added to any song form.)

Verse/chorus/verse/chorus (e.g. "A World Without Family")
Verse/chorus/verse/chorus/bridge/chorus
    (e.g. "You Are What You Eat")
Verse/verse/bridge/verse (e.g. "If I Had a Million Dollars")
Chorus/verse/chorus/verse/chorus
    (e.g. "Dreams and Nightmares")
Verse/verse/chorus/verse/verse/chorus (e.g. "School Spirit")

Emotion & Imagery

Song lyrics are made up of two things—Emotion and Imagery. The chorus usually contains the most emotional words in a song.

Emotional statements evoke feelings. They encourage listeners to care about the characters in the song and, most importantly, make them think about how the lyrics apply to their own lives. I call that "opening the door" for the listener. In "A World Without Family" the chorus uses different examples to show how sad it would be to not have any family. Hopefully, when you listen to that song, you will think about your own family and feel thankful for them.

Imagery is the use of description to make a point or to show an idea. Remember "show me, don't tell me"? For a good example of imagery, check out the two verses in "We're All Different." While the chorus for this song makes a simple statement, the verses go into detail to paint a picture. In the first verse, we compare people to M&Ms to show how we are all different on the outside. In the second verse, we make the point that everyone has a heart and a brain, which makes us all similar on the inside. Can you think of ways to describe how we are all different and the same?

Rhyme

Rhyming is a big part of what makes songs fun to sing and easy to remember. However, rhymes can make it harder for writers to say exactly what they want to say. There's no rule on how much or how little a song should rhyme. Take a look at how the songs in this book rhyme, and try to imitate one of the patterns. Notice how each verse in a song follows the same pattern as the one before it. A fun way to practice is to try to rhyme a one-syllable word with the last syllable of a two- or three-syllable word, like "wait" with "elevate."

Music & Sounds

Songs are more than just lyrics. The right music and sounds are just as important as the words.

In "Dreams and Nightmares," listen to how "dreams" is held out when it is sung, to give the listener a good feeling. On the other hand, the word "nightmares" is sung in a short, sharp way to scare the listener—just like a nightmare would. Likewise, the notes in "My Pets" are quick, light, and cheerful, and for the verses we chose sounds and words that remind us of the animals we're singing about, like a snake that slithers and hisses.

In "A World Without Family," the chorus intentionally sounds sad—just how you might feel if you had no family. "You Are What You Eat" and "School Spirit" are upbeat and fun. If we sang "School Spirit" in a sad or angry tone, it wouldn't sound very spirited. In "The Four Rs," listen to the word "rot." It sounds harsh and kind of gross, and brings to mind the image of something rotting.

If you play an instrument, make up your own chords and melody to go with your words. (A melody is a series of single notes played or sung along with the chords.) If you're not ready for that yet, write your own words to be sung to one of the tunes in the book or to the tunes of one of your favorite songs. There are also four instrumental tracks on the CD that can help you write your words and melody. Track #4 is a version of track #3, but with a melody that you can use if you don't feel like making up your own.

Collaboration

When you write a song, you can do it by yourself or with a friend or someone in your family. Remember, I wrote each song in this book with the help of 30 or more kids. Sometimes it's more fun to work with a big group.

Have Fun!

The most important thing to do when you're writing a song is to put your heart into it and enjoy the process. If you write a song that you believe in, your listeners will be moved to laughter or tears. You can inspire them to think about something in a way they've never considered before. You can make them see things from your perspective. We all have the power to share our stories with the world, and writing a song is a wonderful way to be creative, express yourself, and have fun at the same time.